MW00987208

A YEAR OF SELF-LOVE JOURNAL

A YEAR OF
Self-Love
JOURNAL

52 Weeks of Prompts and Practices for Loving Who You Are

JAMILA I. WHITE

ROCKRIDGE
PRESS

To mom, Ifetayo Jacqueline Scott White,
who lives and loves by example.

And to my grandmothers: Anna, Mother Ruth,
Annie, and Louise. I am because you were.

For general information on our other products and services, please contact our Customer Care Department within the United States at (866) 744-2665, or outside the United States at (510) 253-0500.

Paperback ISBN: 978-1-68539-940-5

Manufactured in the United States of America

Interior and Cover Designer: Keirsten Geise
Art Producer: Hannah Dickerson
Editor: Laura Cerrone
Production Editor: Emily Sheehan
Production Manager: Lanore Coloprisco

All illustrations used under license from Shutterstock.com; author photo courtesy of Steven Cumberbatch

10 9 8 7 6 5 4 3 2 1 0

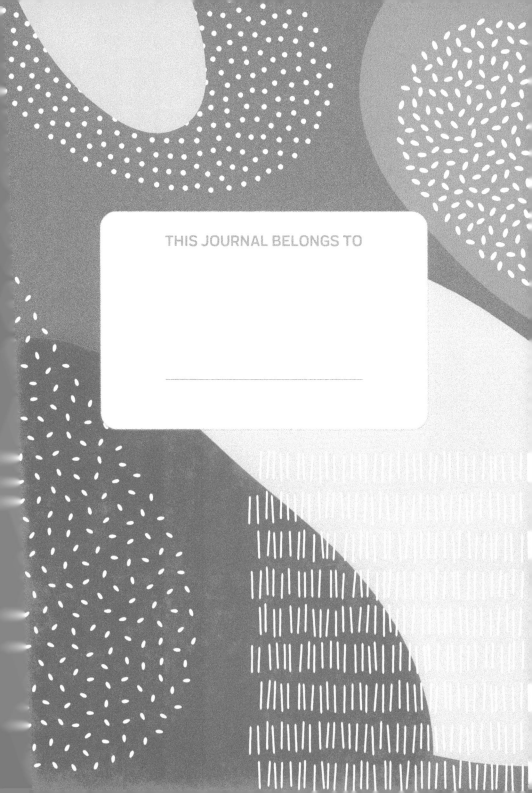

THIS JOURNAL BELONGS TO

_____

TABLE OF CONTENTS

INTRODUCTION

MY JOURNEY TO HELP PEOPLE LOVE and trust themselves started with a simple question from a client.

"*But how* . . . ? Everyone says, 'you need to learn how to love yourself,' but no one says *how* to do it. How do I start loving myself?"

Natasha, who'd been coming to me for intuitive consultations and life coaching, asked me this question as we discussed the root cause of a painful pattern in her romantic relationships.

Her question made me pause.

The work we did together over the next few months would set her on a journey that transformed how she viewed herself and the world around her. Natasha began to focus less on the men in her life, and more on herself, her healing, and her joy. She even changed to a more fulfilling career.

Like Natasha and so many of us, my own journey to self-love began with discomfort. Dark nights of the soul. Also, the questions: *How did I get here? And how do I get out?*

Many people think of physical pampering when they think of self-love. But true self-love goes further than that:

Are you at peace?

Do you love yourself unconditionally?

Can you forgive yourself completely for your mistakes?

Do you really like the person you see in the mirror?

Do you believe you're a good person?

Do you believe you deserve a truly wonderful, joyful life?

So much of learning to love ourselves involves *unlearning* limiting beliefs. Rooting around in the shadows of our hearts and minds to learn where those thoughts about being unworthy, unhappy, and small came from, and, more importantly, replacing them with the Truth (with a capital "T") of who we really are.

A journaling practice is perfect for reflection that uncovers what thoughts, beliefs, and aspirations we hold dear, away from judgment, from other people, and even from ourselves.

Journaling changed my life. I was emotionally spent from being in entrepreneurial hustle mode, "doing all the things," bank account on empty, and feeling stuck. I was also depressed, though it would be years before I would be clinically diagnosed. All I knew was that my life wasn't working.

I was gifted a copy of *The Artist's Way* by Julia Cameron. I got a notebook and reluctantly started writing. Eventually, I began to see and know myself in a way I hadn't before. Frustrated scribbles led to breakthroughs, then to creative ideas and even intuitive "hits." If I missed a morning, I felt "off," and would pick it up at night. I journaled nearly every day for ten years.

Two years ago, I wrote a post on Facebook about ultra-independence, trauma, and self-love. It went viral and was shared and forwarded over 100,000 times on social media. The topic had struck a nerve. People felt seen and understood. And, like I saw in my client years before, *people were hungry to learn how to love themselves.*

My intention with this journal is to gently encourage you to uncover your truths. And to love those truths. All of them.

There are a few truths I'd like to start with:

You are not your trauma.

You are not your mistakes.

You are not your bank account, debt, or credit score.

You are not your insulin level, BMI, or clothing size.

You are not other people's stories about you.

You are not even your limited story about yourself.

You are worthy.

You are worthy.

You are worthy.

You are loved.

I love you.

HOW TO USE THIS JOURNAL

A YEAR OF SELF-LOVE JOURNAL is a guided journal of fifty-two chapters of engaging activities to accompany you through the fifty-two weeks of a year.

Each chapter includes:

- A positive affirmation for you to repeat out loud daily during that week

- Journaling prompts to encourage you to explore and reflect on your feelings, beliefs, and experiences relating to that particular aspect of self-love

- A mind-body-spirit practice to help you embody self-love outside the journal

- An exercise to complete in the journal, such as an introspective worksheet, quiz, or space to create art

Although this journal is designed to go in sequential order from week 1 to week 52, this is *your* self-love journey. You get to decide if you'd like to work through it from start to finish with one chapter per week, or if you'd prefer to visit chapters according to the themes you're most drawn to in a particular week.

At the end of each quarter, there's a "check-in" week to assist you with honoring your progress and reflecting on your journey up to that point.

GETTING THE MOST OF THIS JOURNAL

◇◇◇

THE PROCESS IS SIMPLE—YOU'LL GET from this journal what you put into it!

This is your journey. This is your commitment to yourself to break through the doubts and fears that have been standing in the way of you accepting and loving yourself unconditionally. You're not here to love me; you're here to love *you*!

It may feel challenging at first to go deeper and explore some of the nooks and crannies in your heart. At times you will feel encouraged and inspired; at other times you may feel a bit uncomfortable as you examine your relationship with yourself. Stick with it; the reward of loving yourself better is so worth it!

Here are some tips to help you stay on track:

- **Make a regular appointment with yourself.** Write in your calendar when you plan to journal. My suggestion is to start with one hour per week, which you can break up into smaller fifteen- or thirty-minute chunks throughout the week and adjust as you get a better sense of your time needs.

- **Create a special place for your journaling activities.** Ideally, choose a quiet place where you can have uninterrupted time with yourself for a little while. Make the space personal and cozy. Consider adding a candle, flowers, or an object that's special or inspiring to you.

- **Life happens. If you miss a week, pick up where you left off and keep going.** More important than sticking to a schedule is the momentum of moving forward. Don't let your inner critic judge and beat up on you. Be kind with yourself. Tell the critic *hush!* and get back to journaling.

- **Stay open.** Be present for whatever comes up for you while journaling. Be gentle with yourself and show yourself love and compassion if any tough feelings come up. And, celebrate when you have a breakthrough or an *a-ha* moment!

- **Have fun!** Feel free to doodle, color, or add stickers to your journal if it makes you feel good.

- **Get support.** Pair up with a friend who is also doing *A Year of Self-Love Journal* to encourage and support each other on your self-love journey. Join me and other like-hearted souls who are rocking their journals in the official support community at www.ayearofselflove.com. (It's free!)

I'm rooting for you!

PROGRESS TRACKER

Keep track of your self-love journey by placing a checkmark next to each week that you complete.

___ Week 1	___ Week 19	___ Week 37
___ Week 2	___ Week 20	___ Week 38
___ Week 3	___ Week 21	___ Week 39
___ Week 4	___ Week 22	___ Week 40
___ Week 5	___ Week 23	___ Week 41
___ Week 6	___ Week 24	___ Week 42
___ Week 7	___ Week 25	___ Week 43
___ Week 8	___ Week 26	___ Week 44
___ Week 9	___ Week 27	___ Week 45
___ Week 10	___ Week 28	___ Week 46
___ Week 11	___ Week 29	___ Week 47
___ Week 12	___ Week 30	___ Week 48
___ Week 13	___ Week 31	___ Week 49
___ Week 14	___ Week 32	___ Week 50
___ Week 15	___ Week 33	___ Week 51
___ Week 16	___ Week 34	___ Week 52
___ Week 17	___ Week 35	
___ Week 18	___ Week 36	

WEEK 1

I am willing to learn how to love myself.
I am worthy of unconditional love.

What made you start this self-love journal? What do you hope to accomplish or shift by journaling? What's your biggest obstacle when it comes to self-love?

_____

_____

_____

_____

_____

If you truly loved and accepted all parts of yourself, who could you be? What specifically would you be able to do? How would your life be better, and how would you be happier?

_____

_____

_____

_____

_____

_____

READY TO TRY

The words we speak have power. You can use the power of your words to open your heart and begin not only seeing yourself as worthy but also walking in your worthiness.

Take three deep breaths, slowly inhaling and exhaling. Place your hands over your heart and say:

I, _____ , commit to learning how to love myself. I am willing to grow, see, and accept myself completely. I am willing to learn how to love all of me, not only the parts I feel are wonderful, but also the wounded parts, the not-so-great parts, and everything in between. Change starts with me. I am ready to believe in myself. I am worthy. I am worthy. I am worthy.

TAKING STOCK

Getting a sense of where you are at the beginning of your year of self-love will help you notice your progress throughout your journey. Circle the number that describes how much you disagree (0) or agree (5) with each statement below:

I really love myself.

0   1   2   3   4   5

I have many positive qualities.

0   1   2   3   4   5

I practice self-care regularly.

0   1   2   3   4   5

I feel worthy of love.

0   1   2   3   4   5

I am a good person.

0   1   2   3   4   5

I have the power to create positive change in my life.

0   1   2   3   4   5

I make good decisions.

0   1   2   3   4   5

I like how I look.

0   1   2   3   4   5

I honor and maintain healthy boundaries.

0   1   2   3   4   5

I deserve a good life.

0   1   2   3   4   5

I have healthy relationships.

0   1   2   3   4   5

Add up the total for every number circled.

TOTAL SCORE: _____

If you scored:

0 to 11: You're in the right place; you have a great opportunity to start loving yourself and building up your sense of self-worth. This journal will help you do just that.

12 to 22: You're open to self-love. The practices in this book will help you gain self-confidence and become more aware of how to be more loving with yourself.

23 to 33: You have a fairly healthy relationship with yourself. An intentional and consistent self-love and self-care practice will help you strengthen it further.

34 or more: You're well connected to your heart and have been loving yourself well. Keep going!

WEEK 2

I am creating a new relationship with my
body based on love and appreciation.

What's a recollection of someone commenting on your body's size, shape, facial features, height, etc.? Perhaps this comment even came from within. How did that feel? Does it influence how you think about your body today? How?

_____

_____

_____

_____

_____

What do you appreciate most about your body? Describe one positive memory where your body's involvement was central to the experience. (Example: dancing at a loved one's wedding)

_____

_____

_____

_____

_____

SPEAK LOVE TO YOUR BODY

Loving ourselves more deeply sometimes means getting to know ourselves in ways we haven't before. Today, listen to what your body needs from you.

1. Close your eyes and place your hands over your heart.

2. Take three deep, slow breaths.

3. Ask your body: *What do you need to hear from me to feel loved?*

4. Listen with your heart for the answer. Speak those words out loud to your body.

LOVE YOUR BODY!

Celebrate your body three ways this week.
   Ideas (feel free to add your own):

- Admire your body in the mirror.

- Relax in a warm bath.

- Draw hearts on your least favorite body part with a non-toxic marker.

- Pamper yourself with a massage or Reiki energy healing session.

- Throw yourself a ten-minute dance party.

- _____

- _____

- _____

- _____

Action	★
1.	
2.	
3.	

WEEK 3

I am worthy of the same compassion and
kindness I generously give to others.

Sometimes we judge ourselves more harshly than we'd ever judge
a loved one. What are some ways you criticize yourself when
you're facing a challenge or experiencing a difficult season in
your life?

_____

_____

_____

_____

_____

_____

_____

_____

_____

_____

_____

_____

_____

If your best friend, family member, or other loved one was going through a tough time and felt afraid, ashamed, overwhelmed, discouraged, or hopeless, what might you say to offer support and encouragement?

_____

_____

_____

_____

_____

_____

_____

_____

_____

_____

CREATE YOUR OWN GREETING CARDS

Using paper and markers or your computer, create some encouraging greeting cards—for yourself!

1. Draw colorful images or use uplifting clip art on the outside.

2. Fold the paper in half and write an encouraging message to yourself on the inside. For inspiration, feel free to use phrases from your journaling prompts or affirmations throughout the book.

3. Display a few where you can see them, and stash the others nearby for future encouragement.

I AM . . .

Circle the "I am" words in the puzzle below. They may appear horizontally, vertically, or diagonally. How many can you find?

```
R  T  G  R  A  T  E  F  U  L  X  P  D  T  I  X  G  H  C  W
L  H  O  P  E  F  U  L  I  F  N  L  E  A  R  N  I  N  G  O
Q  U  R  U  X  F  O  S  O  L  A  R  E  R  T  X  L  L  I  R
S  M  W  I  A  N  E  H  M  Y  D  Q  D  R  G  V  C  C  U  T
M  T  I  A  L  O  V  A  B  L  E  J  I  E  A  B  S  V  E  H
A  F  U  N  N  Y  W  R  R  H  B  I  N  S  P  I  R  E  D  Y
R  S  U  C  Q  G  U  G  C  L  M  E  J  N  D  C  V  K  D  U
T  I  D  L  W  J  P  D  G  H  E  R  A  E  N  O  U  G  H  L
B  S  N  Y  I  S  U  C  C  E  S  S  F  U  L  T  W  N  B  C
F  R  Z  P  R  E  S  E  N  T  K  H  S  I  T  O  I  A  R  O
C  C  I  V  G  Z  S  P  M  S  C  Z  R  V  A  I  G  G  A  N
I  A  D  L  A  W  P  O  W  E  R  F  U  L  P  P  F  H  V  F
C  B  P  K  L  L  R  E  S  O  U  R  C  E  F  U  L  U  E  I
Q  R  D  A  E  I  U  S  A  W  E  S  O  M  E  L  K  J  L  D
O  L  E  D  B  P  A  A  B  R  G  V  S  G  D  J  Q  K  S  E
Y  E  N  A  U  L  R  N  B  E  G  X  M  W  N  E  B  J  T  N
U  X  B  H  T  K  E  O  T  L  M  L  O  V  I  N  G  T  R  T
Y  D  A  H  Z  I  Y  C  U  J  E  D  A  T  M  L  C  W  O  N
L  O  V  E  D  N  V  I  O  D  V  R  E  S  I  L  I  E  N  T
M  V  V  F  B  D  Q  E  S  N  Q  C  U  J  Z  T  X  V  G  P
```

Answer key on page 12

Awesome	Creative	Inspired	Powerful	Strong
Beautiful	Enough	Kind	Present	Successful
Brave	Fearless	Learning	Proud	Valuable
Brilliant	Funny	Lovable	Resilient	Worthy
Capable	Grateful	Loved	Resourceful	
Confident	Hopeful	Loving	Smart	

```
R T G R A T E F U L X P D T I X G H C W
L H O P E F U L I F N L E A R N I N G O
Q U R U X F O S O L A R E R T X L L I R
S M W I A N E H M Y D Q D R G V C C U T
M T I A L O V A B L E J I E A B S V E H
A F U N N Y W R R H B I N S P I R E D Y
R S U C Q G U G C L M E J N D C V K D U
T I D L W J P D G H E R A E N O U G H L
B S N Y I S U C C E S S F U L T W N B C
F R Z P R E S E N T K H S I T O I A R O
C C I V G Z S P M S C Z R V A I G G A N
I A D L A W P O W E R F U L P P F H V F
C B P K L L R E S O U R C E F U L U E I
Q R D A E I U S A W E S O M E L K J L D
O L E D B P A A B R G V S G D J Q K S E
Y E N A U L R N B E G X M W N E B J T N
U X B H T K E O T L M L O V I N G T R T
Y D A H Z I Y C U J E D A T M L C W O N
L O V E D N V I O D V R E S I L I E N T
M V V F B D Q E S N Q C U J Z T X V G P
```

WEEK 4

My greatest power is my ability to choose.
I trust myself to make good decisions.

Think of a time you felt you had made a "bad" decision or a choice that backfired. What did you learn from it? Now that you're wiser, how might you choose differently today?

_____

_____

_____

_____

_____

What are some big decisions you've made that turned out well? Have you made any recent small choices that show love and compassion for yourself? Describe them.

_____

_____

_____

_____

_____

_____

FORGIVING MY PAST CHOICES

You may sometimes judge and punish yourself over past decisions you came to regret. Forgiving and releasing this judgment is a form of self-love.

1. Find a quiet place; perhaps light a candle.

2. Take a few deep breaths.

3. Say aloud:

I, _____ , now fully and forever forgive myself for _____ . Although I know differently now, I recognize it was the best I could do and the choice that felt the safest to me at that time. I am now ready to trust myself to make good decisions.

RECLAIMING MY POWER

Reframing circumstances as choices helps you remember how powerful you are, and it grows your awareness about opportunities to exercise this power. When you feel powerless, remember your power of choice.

Circumstance	*My Choice*
I have to . . .	**Instead: I choose to . . .**
Ex: I have to go to work.	*Instead: I choose to provide for my family.*

1. _____

    Instead:_____

2. _____

   Instead:_____

3. _____

   Instead:_____

4. _____

   Instead:_____

5. _____

   Instead:_____

WEEK 5

I deserve to rest. I honor my body, mind, and
spirit by regularly replenishing my energy.

Rest isn't a reward for a job well done; ongoing rest is a necessary
and important form of self-love and self-care. On a scale of 1 to 10,
with 1 being "completely exhausted" and 10 being "fully rested,"
how rested do you feel today? Why?

_____

_____

_____

_____

_____

Do you ever feel lazy or guilty for taking time to rest? What did you
learn growing up about hard work, productivity, and staying busy?
About rest?

_____

_____

_____

_____

_____

CREATE A REST RITUAL

Even when we are busiest, it's important to stop and rest. Taking a cue from Reclaiming My Power on page 14, remember that you have the power to choose. Today, use that power to restore your energy.

1. During a break in your day, find a quiet, dimly lit location.

2. For twenty minutes, take a nap. Or sit quietly with your eyes closed and focus on your breathing for twenty minutes.

3. If you have trouble settling down, consider inhaling a few drops of pure lavender essential oil on a tissue or listening to a binaural beats sleep program (there are many free ones on YouTube) with noise-canceling headphones.

TRACK YOUR SLEEP

Giving ourselves rest is one way we love ourselves. We don't expect our phones to work well without recharging their batteries, and our minds and bodies need to recharge, too. This week, fill out the chart on the following pages with your sleep information.

How many hours of sleep each night would make you feel fully rested? This week, track how much and the quality of sleep you get:

	Start Time	End Time	Total Hours	Quality 1= worst; 10= best	Notes
Ex.	11:00 p.m.	6:30 a.m.	7.5	8	
Sun					
Mon					
Tues					

Wed					
Thurs					
Fri					
Sat					
Total Hours					

Reflections about your sleep this week (pay attention to the notes you took):

_____

_____

WEEK 6

I am worthy of being celebrated, especially on my
birthday. My arrival in this world was a big deal!

How were birthdays observed in your family or culture growing
up? What feelings come up for you when you reflect on your childhood birthdays? What feelings come up when you think of your
next birthday?

_____

_____

_____

_____

_____

Describe your ideal birthday. How would you start your day? How
would you spend the day? With whom would you spend it? Where
would you go, and what would you do?

_____

_____

_____

_____

_____

BIRTHDAY FEELINGS MEDITATION

1. Take three deep, slow breaths.

2. Meditate on turning ten years older than you are now.

3. As you breathe, notice what feelings arise and where in your body you feel them.

4. Pay close attention to any places you feel tension, fear, or heaviness. Breathe into those places and release the feelings.

5. Next, breathe in love for the wisdom and experience you will have, then breathe out any tension.

MY BIRTHDAY VISION BOARD

Pretend today is your birthday (or maybe it is!). Think about how you'd like to feel and what you'd like to do to celebrate your next year of life. Find five to ten images that depict the vibe, activities, and aspirations. Cut pictures and words from magazines and paste them in the space provided on the next page or find images online and use a free online vision board tool to arrange them.

MY BIRTHDAY VISION BOARD WORK SPACE

WEEK 7

Is it easy for you to ask for or accept help? Why or why not? Do you trust others to help you? What experiences and beliefs sometimes prevent you from asking for help?

_____

_____

_____

_____

_____

_____

Where in your life do you currently feel overwhelmed? Who could you ask for help or support? How might having more support free up your time and energy?

_____

_____

_____

_____

MAGIC HELPER VISUALIZATION

Imagine you have a Magical Helper—an angel, fairy godmother, robot, or even an animal—devoted to assisting *you*. Your Magical Helper is at your service, ready to assist with anything you need. Tune in to your heart. What do you most need help with right now? Ask your Magical Helper to help you out, the way you'd ask someone you trust! Visualize how this would play out.

GETTING SUPPORT

List your most pressing tasks or responsibilities in the column on the left. Which tasks aren't truly necessary and can be eliminated altogether? What can you get help doing, and who can help? What can you assign to someone else? If it's a task or situation that needs a miracle, delegate it to a higher power—pray, meditate, sit with nature—whatever works for you! Release your attachment to the outcome, and watch to see how it gets resolved.

Keep track of your thoughts on the lines below as you fill out the chart on the next page.

_____

_____

_____

_____

_____

_____

_____

_____

_____

Complete the chart, then schedule time this week to address each task.

Task	Eliminate ✓	Do Together With:	Delegate To:	Delegate to Higher Power ✓
Ex: **Kids' laundry**			Kids	

WEEK 8

I am lovable. I am worth loving. I am easy to love.

You may struggle to love yourself. What parts of you do you feel are most challenging to love? What do you think it would take for you to love these parts of yourself?

_____

_____

_____

_____

_____

_____

Recall a time when you felt loved. How did you know that you were loved; what behaviors helped you identify the feeling as "loved"? Can you use some of those behaviors to love yourself? If so, how?

_____

_____

_____

_____

_____

_____

MIRROR WORK

Speaking positively to yourself in a mirror on a regular basis can have a tremendous impact on your self-esteem and help you become more aware of where you may be resisting seeing and thinking of yourself in a positive light.

1. In front of a mirror, take a few deep, slow breaths.

2. Look yourself in the eyes and say:

    I love you, _____ (your name).
    You are easy to love.
    You are worthy of unconditional love.

3. Repeat these sentences five times. Notice how it feels to say them, and observe without judgment any feelings of resistance, discomfort, or "this feels silly."

WHO LOVES YA, BABY?

Make a list of everyone who has ever loved you. Your list may include people, a higher power, pets–anyone. When you feel doubtful, unloved, or unappreciated, pull out this list as a reminder that you are indeed lovable!

_____   _____

_____   _____

_____   _____

_____   _____

_____   _____

_____   _____

WEEK 9

My energy is valuable. I am willing to
say no to whatever drains me so I can
say yes to what matters most.

What and who are your biggest energy drains? Do you sometimes say yes to things that your spirit wants you to say no to? If yes, why do you think you hesitate to speak up?

_____

_____

_____

_____

_____

If you are completely honest with yourself, what would you really like to say no to? If you got rid of the situations that drain you, what would you then have the time and energy to do?

_____

_____

_____

_____

_____

PAUSE BEFORE ANSWERING

If you tend to immediately say yes to a request and then regret it later, this practice can help you answer in a more empowered and authentic way.

1. **Pause.** When someone makes a request of you, resist the urge to automatically say yes, and pause. Give yourself time to reflect. If possible, ask for more time: "I'll get back to you on that."

2. **Check in with yourself.** Ask yourself if you have both the *desire* and the *capacity* to say yes. Is this something you want to do? How to tell if it's a no: If it isn't a whole-body *yes* that resonates with your spirit, it's a *no*. If it's fuzzy, if it's a maybe, or if you aren't sure, then it's also a *no*.

Although "no" is a complete sentence that doesn't always need justification, here are some other ways to say no. Practice saying them out loud now, so it's easier to say in a real situation:

"Not at this time."

"No, I'd rather _____ ."

"Hmm. That doesn't feel right to me right now. Can I support you in a different way?"

"No, thanks."

"Let's reschedule."

"I'd like to go in a different direction."

"This doesn't work for me anymore."

"Going forward, the way I'm going to do this is _____ ."

Write your own responses:

_____

_____

_____

GET CLEAR WITH YOURSELF

Take a few deep breaths and check in with yourself, then complete the following worksheet.

Five Things I Need to Say No To:

1. _____

2. _____

3. _____

4. _____

5. _____

Five Things I Want to Say Yes To:

1. _____

2. _____

3. _____

4. _____

5. _____

WEEK 10

Intuition is like a muscle. The more you use it, the stronger and clearer it gets. Describe a time when you trusted your intuition and then acted on it.

_____

_____

_____

_____

_____

Have you ever picked up weird "vibes" or even specific information about a person or situation? What did you do with this information? What guidance have you gotten throughout your life about trusting your intuition?

_____

_____

_____

_____

_____

_____

INTUITIVE NATURE WALK

Today, take a nature walk, or watch a nature video online, with your phone on silent.

1. As you walk (or view the video), take deep, slow breaths.

2. Be present to your surroundings (or the video). What do you see? What do you hear (or imagine you hear)? How does the earth feel (or how do you think it feels)? What do you smell and taste (or imagine)?

3. After ten minutes, breathe and ask yourself: *In this moment, what do I know?*

4. Listen without judgment for the answer.

HOW INTUITIVE ARE YOU?

Circle the number that describes how much you disagree (0) or agree (5) with each statement below:

I sometimes feel confident about a decision or situation that makes no logical sense.

0   1   2   3   4   5

I have vivid and sometimes prophetic dreams.

0   1   2   3   4   5

I pick up on the emotions or vibes of others.

0   1   2   3   4   5

Sometimes I "just know" something and don't know how I know it.

O   1   2   3   4   5

I've thought of someone and then received a text or call from them soon after.

O   1   2   3   4   5

I feel something in my body, like tightness in my chest or butter-flies in my stomach, when something is wrong.

O   1   2   3   4   5

I notice a lot of synchronicities (meaningful coincidences).

O   1   2   3   4   5

I've had premonitions about things that later came to pass.

O   1   2   3   4   5

I sometimes feel uneasy about a decision or situation when no one else around me does.

O   1   2   3   4   5

Sometimes I suddenly receive or "download" ideas, thoughts, or complete concepts.

O   1   2   3   4   5

Add up the total for every number circled.

TOTAL SCORE: _____

If you scored:

0 to 12: Your intuition is trying to get your attention—be open to your inner guidance. Consider exploring any limiting beliefs you may have learned from family, school, religion, or elsewhere about trusting your intuition.

13 to 25: You're awakened to your intuition. Cultivate it by intentionally observing synchronicities around you and tuning in to your body.

26 to 38: You have a healthy relationship with your intuition. Strengthen it with meditation and regularly journaling your observations and reflections.

39 or more: You have a great relationship with your intuition. Keep going!

WEEK 11

My intuition reveals what I need to
know at just the right moment.

Describe a time when you didn't trust your intuition. How did your
intuition show up? What made you hesitate or disregard what
you felt?

_____

_____

_____

_____

_____

Recall a time when you knew something intuitively and trusted it.
What happened, and what was the result? How did you know your
intuition was working then? What made you trust yourself?

_____

_____

_____

_____

_____

_____

AUTOMATIC WRITING

Take some time today to allow your intuition to come forth. Writing without judgment can help even hidden thoughts spill out onto paper.

1. Grab a pen and paper or a journal. Write a question about a situation you'd like your intuition to help you with on a piece of paper or in a journal. A single, open-ended question is better than a yes or no question.

2. Clear your mind by breathing slowly for a few minutes.

3. Gently touch your pen to the paper.

4. Relax your hand, and without thinking about it allow yourself to write. Let any words, images, or symbols flow onto the paper. Take your time and don't worry if anything doesn't come right away.

5. When it feels done, reflect on what's on the paper.

You may need to try this a few times. With practice, it gets easier.

KEEP AN INTUITION DIARY

Each day this week, pay close attention to your dreams, feelings, hunches, body sensations, and coincidences. Don't judge or try to interpret; just observe. On the following pages, jot down whatever thoughts arise. Each day, review the entries from the previous days.

Sunday: _____

_____

_____

_____

_____

Monday: _____

_____

_____

_____

_____

Tuesday: _____

_____

_____

_____

_____

Wednesday: _____

_____

_____

_____

_____

Thursday: _____

_____

_____

_____

_____

_____

Friday: _____

_____

_____

_____

_____

_____

Saturday: _____

_____

_____

_____

_____

_____

At the end of the week, answer these questions:

1. How did your intuition show up for you?

_____

_____

_____

_____

_____

2. Did you notice any patterns?

_____

_____

_____

_____

_____

3. Did anything that came up earlier in the week make sense later in the week? If so, what?

_____

_____

_____

_____

_____

WEEK 12

I have a great sense of humor. I deserve a life
filled with lighthearted fun and laughter.

Laughter is beneficial to the body, mind, and spirit. Write about the
last time you laughed really hard. What memory makes you laugh
every time you think about it?

_____

_____

_____

_____

_____

Recall a time when you were able to find humor during a difficult
experience. What did you do? Is there a current situation you can
bring more lightheartedness to?

_____

_____

_____

_____

_____

_____

LOL

Admittedly, laughing comes easier for some people than others. But did you know you can enjoy the benefits of natural laughter by laughing at will? It's true. Give this practice a try, and notice how it lifts your spirits.

1. Visualize a laugh inside your heart.

2. Smile, first small, then as widely as you can.

3. As your smile grows, allow the laughter to escape from your heart and into a giggle and rise to soft laughter.

4. Play with the sound, switching to a higher or lower pitch and louder volume, until you are cracking up!

MY FUNNY WEEK

Engage in one laugh-inducing activity each day this week. Choose from the list below or create your own. Record what you did each day and how it made you feel.

- Get a fun toy for your desk or nightstand.

- Go to a live comedy show.

- Imitate your favorite celebrity's or character's laugh.

- Play with young children.

- Talk with someone who makes you laugh.

- Read a book of jokes.

- Read a comic strip.

- Share a funny memory with a friend.

- Switch your computer screensaver to a funny picture.

- Take an improv class.
- Tell a joke.
- Watch a stand-up comedy special on TV or the internet.
- Watch a funny movie or TV show.
- _____
- _____
- _____
- _____
- _____
- _____

Sunday: _____

Monday: _____

Tuesday: _____

Wednesday: _____

Thursday: _____

Friday: _____

Saturday: _____

WEEK 13

I love watching myself evolve and grow, and I honor
my progress. I'm on my way to truly loving me.

Hey now! You're a quarter of the way through your year of self-love.
Let's check in: How are you feeling about yourself today? Which
practices and exercises from this journal have you found most
useful so far? Why?

_____

_____

_____

_____

_____

How easy or challenging has it been to be consistent with your
journaling? If it's easy, what habits have helped you stay on track?
If it's challenging, what obstacles have affected your consis-
tency? What could you do to journal more regularly?

_____

_____

_____

_____

_____

YOGA STAR POSE

Yoga poses can help balance the mind, body, and spirit. *Utthita tadasana*, known as the Star pose, opens your heart to more compassion, love, and forgiveness.

1. Stand upright with legs spread wide, toes facing front.

2. Stretch your arms out evenly, palms facing down and fingers open.

3. Breathe deeply, then gently lengthen your torso, reach your hands out further, and stretch the top of your head toward the sky. Look straight ahead.

4. If you can, gently hold the pose for one minute.

FIRST-QUARTER CHECK-IN

Check in with yourself and reflect on what you've discovered since you started this journal.

Complete the sentences below:

Something I noticed about myself is _____

_____

_____

_____

I'm starting to see a change with _____

_____

_____

_____

My favorite affirmation right now is _____

_____

_____

_____

Something I'd like to release is _____

_____

_____

_____

WEEK 14

I focus on what is in my control, and
release what is not mine to carry.

Part of self-love is managing what you give your attention to—both within you and around you. In what ways do you feel responsible for the behavior, feelings, thoughts, ideas, and decisions of other people?

_____

_____

_____

_____

_____

How would it feel to free yourself from carrying what isn't yours? What would you have the energy to do? What in your life would change as a result?

_____

_____

_____

_____

_____

YOGA SHOULDER STRETCH

This stretch will help relieve tension in your shoulders, a common area where we hold stress.

1. While sitting or standing, relax your shoulders.

2. Reach your right arm across your chest at shoulder height.

3. Use your left arm to gently pull it closer against your chest and hold for about one minute.

4. Release, and switch arms.

5. Repeat as needed.

Check off the items below that seem to be an issue for you, then read the direction that follows.

Things I can control:

___ My positive attitude

___ How I speak to myself

___ How I speak to others

___ What I give my attention to

___ My self-care

___ My choices

___ What I eat

___ The boundaries I set and maintain

___ How much sleep I get

___ Asking for help

___ How much news I consume, and where I consume it

___ How much time I spend on social media, and which accounts I follow

___ How I honor my word

Things I cannot control:

___ The weather

___ How others act

___ Other people's choices

___ How other people react

___ The traffic

___ The past

___ The future

This week, look for opportunities to redirect your focus from things you can't control to things you can.

WEEK 15

I walk in my gifts, even if I don't know where
they will lead. My gifts will make room for me.

Sometimes we don't recognize our gifts because they come easily
to us. What skills, talents, and gifts do you have? What tasks are
you good at? What do people praise you for, ask you to help them
with, or ask you to explain to them?

_____

_____

_____

_____

_____

Reflect on your childhood interests and talents. Explore whether
you felt fully encouraged and supported to pursue them without
judgment. What feelings come up when you think about sharing
your talents with others now?

_____

_____

_____

_____

_____

AFFIRM YOUR CHILDHOOD SELF

1. Focus on a photo of yourself as a child.

2. Take a deep breath, look into your eyes in the photo, and say out loud:

You matter and your gifts are valuable, even if others don't see their value or say they aren't practical. You deserve every opportunity to explore, engage, and shine. It is safe to trust the guidance of your heart. I give you permission to follow your curiosity and passions, today and always.

USING MY GIFTS

On a scale of 1 to 5, with 1 being *strongly disagree* and 5 being *strongly agree*, circle the number that best describes how you feel:

I am passionate about my current occupation, school major, or calling in life.

1   2   3   4   5

I have a hobby or profession that gives me a strong sense of purpose or satisfaction.

1   2   3   4   5

I have people in my life now who are supportive of my talents and interests.

1   2   3   4   5

WEEK 16

Think about something you've come to love about yourself now that you didn't love when you were younger. Write about what caused this shift in your perspective.

_____

_____

_____

_____

_____

Being completely honest, what parts of yourself are you struggling to love? How might you feel about them ten years from now? What would need to happen to make that shift?

_____

_____

_____

_____

_____

_____

GLOWING HEART MEDITATION

1. Close your eyes.

2. Take three slow, deep breaths.

3. Place your hands over your heart and continue breathing deeply.

4. Visualize your breath going into your heart.

5. See your heart begin to glow, first faintly, then glowing brighter with every inhale.

6. Visualize the glow emanating from your heart and gradually illuminating your entire body.

7. When you're ready, open your eyes.

8. Reflect on how you feel.

LOVING MY AWESOME SELF

Reflect on what you like and love about yourself, then complete the following sentences:

I love myself most when ⎯⎯⎯⎯⎯⎯⎯⎯⎯⎯⎯⎯⎯⎯⎯⎯⎯⎯⎯⎯⎯

One awesome thing about me is ⎯⎯⎯⎯⎯⎯⎯⎯⎯⎯⎯⎯⎯⎯⎯⎯⎯

I love that I am ⎯⎯⎯⎯⎯⎯⎯⎯⎯⎯⎯⎯⎯⎯⎯⎯⎯⎯⎯⎯⎯⎯⎯

I am most proud of myself when ⎯⎯⎯⎯⎯⎯⎯⎯⎯⎯⎯⎯⎯⎯⎯⎯

⎯⎯⎯⎯⎯⎯⎯⎯⎯⎯⎯⎯⎯⎯⎯⎯⎯⎯⎯⎯⎯⎯⎯⎯⎯⎯⎯⎯⎯⎯⎯⎯

⎯⎯⎯⎯⎯⎯⎯⎯⎯⎯⎯⎯⎯⎯⎯⎯⎯⎯⎯⎯⎯⎯⎯⎯⎯⎯⎯⎯⎯⎯⎯⎯

⎯⎯⎯⎯⎯⎯⎯⎯⎯⎯⎯⎯⎯⎯⎯⎯⎯⎯⎯⎯⎯⎯⎯⎯⎯⎯⎯⎯⎯⎯⎯⎯

I am learning to love my ⎯⎯⎯⎯⎯⎯⎯⎯⎯⎯⎯⎯⎯⎯⎯⎯⎯⎯⎯

WEEK 17

I release what "should've been" and fully
embrace with gratitude the life I have today.

Grief isn't only for the loss of a person or pet. What losses are
you mourning? What's something you thought was supposed to
happen in your life but didn't turn out as expected, or at all?

_____

_____

_____

_____

_____

What are some benefits of the path your life ended up taking?
Were there any pleasant surprises? What aspects of your life are
you most grateful for today?

_____

_____

_____

_____

_____

_____

BUBBLE RELEASE RITUAL

1. Get a bottle of bubbles.

2. On a piece of paper, write down (without judging) all the things–big and small–that should've happened in your life but didn't.

3. Take a deep breath, slowly blow one bubble, and say, "I now release _____ ." As you watch the bubble float away and pop, release that thing forever. Repeat for every item on your list.

4. Feel free to repeat this practice, this time releasing all the things that happened that you regret.

PLOT TWIST!

You are the author of your life story. Think of three times that something in your life took an unexpected or unpleasant turn. Reframe what happened next and write a new, different ending for each one. Get as silly or adventurous as you want!

What Happened		New Ending
1.	Plot Twist! →	

Continued→

What Happened		New Ending
2.	Plot Twist! →	
3.	Plot Twist! →	

WEEK 18

I give myself permission to change my
mind. As I evolve, it's okay for my needs
and desires to evolve as well.

You aren't who you were yesterday, and it's perfectly normal to change your mind as you grow. What are some things you wish you could change your mind about?

_____

_____

_____

_____

_____

Think about the thoughts and emotions that arise when you think about changing your mind. What do you fear will happen? What good will happen? What will happen to your heart if you don't make the change?

_____

_____

_____

_____

_____

MINDFUL TRANSITIONS

Throughout the day, notice all the small ways your focus changes. When it's time to end one activity or task, pause and honor its completion before starting the next. For example, after you wake up in the morning, after you complete a work task, or after you eat, take a thirty-second pause. Breathe, and say, "This is finished." Then move on to the next activity.

ZAPPING LIMITING BELIEFS

Becoming more aware of any limiting beliefs you hold will help you release them.

Check off the thoughts below that arose for you when completing the journal prompts this week, or that resonate with you now:

___ I've made my bed and now I have to lie in it.

___ I already paid for it, so I have to use it.

___ I'm too old to start over.

___ I've never seen anyone do it before.

___ People will think I'm a quitter.

___ It's who I've always been.

___ I will seem flaky or unfocused if I change my mind.

___ People like me don't do things like that.

___ But it's always been this way.

___ I don't want to rock the boat.

Remember, you are not your beliefs! A belief is just a thought you continue to think over and over. You have the power to create a new thought and a new belief.

WEEK 19

Reflect on the aspects of your life that feel easy right now. Where do you feel "in the flow?" What skills or talents come easily or naturally to you?

_____

_____

_____

_____

_____

Consider the areas of your life where you may feel stuck. What feels hard or burdensome to do? How might you invite more ease and flow to these stuck or challenging parts?

_____

_____

_____

_____

_____

_____

TAKE YOUR TIME

Commit to a day without rushing.

1. Wake up ten minutes earlier.

2. Take three of those minutes to visualize your day unfolding with ease from start to finish.

3. As you move through the day, notice when you feel rushed or harried. Pause, breathe, then *slow down*.

4. When others make requests of you, pause and, before committing, ask yourself: *Do I have the time and energy to do this?*

5. When scheduling, add enough time in between each meeting or task to regroup from the previous task, prepare, eat, freshen up, and travel from point A to point B at a relaxed pace.

EASY DOES IT

You can experience more ease in your life by appreciating the ease that already exists.

Complete the sentences below at the end of the day.

The easiest part of my day today was

_____

Something that would make things easier for me in my work is

_____

Something that would make things easier for me in my home is

_____

One thing I can take off my plate right now is

_____

WEEK 20

Think about the "cheerleaders" in your life—those who offer you consistent encouragement. What do they say or do that makes you feel supported and valued?

_____

_____

_____

_____

_____

In what ways do you wish you had more emotional support? How comfortable are you asking for emotional support? Consider how your past experiences have influenced that.

_____

_____

_____

_____

_____

_____

POWER PLAYLIST

Make a playlist of songs that make you feel powerful, like you can do anything and you are unstoppable. Listen to it each morning this week and pay attention to how you feel afterward. Short on ideas? Try some of these songs:

- "Break My Stride" by Matthew Wilder
- "Conqueror" by Estelle
- "I'm Every Woman" by Chaka Khan
- "Lose Yourself" by Eminem
- "Rise Up" by Andra Day
- "This Is Me" by Keala Settle and The Greatest Showman Ensemble
- "Unstoppable" by Sia

WRITE AN APPRECIATION LETTER

A letter of appreciation is a powerful way to grow gratitude and give yourself (and another person) a positive boost.

Think about the people in your life, past or present, who have been supportive of you. Choose one of these people and write a letter sharing the ways they have been there for you and what it means to you. Tell them how much you appreciate what they do or did. Consider writing it by hand.

Also consider if you want to share the letter with the other person, and, if so, whether in person (where you get to share the moment with them as they read it), by mail, or by email.

Use the next page to organize your thoughts:

Who:

_____

How They Support(ed) Me:

_____

_____

_____

_____

_____

_____

_____

Why This Support Matters:

_____

_____

_____

_____

_____

_____

_____

WEEK 21

I belong here. I am more than enough. I am
worthy to have a seat at this table.

Impostor syndrome is when you feel like a fraud or that you aren't good enough, in spite of your accomplishments, education, or experience. Describe a time when you felt this way. What do you think caused your self-doubt?

_____

_____

_____

_____

_____

Consider the skills, qualities, and achievements that have led to where you are now. What would a trusted friend or colleague say to you to encourage you?

_____

_____

_____

_____

_____

POSITIVE SELF-TALK

It's normal to have doubts when you're faced with a new situation, or something didn't go your way. When negative or judgmental thoughts come up, replace them with positive self-talk.

Review the following examples of replacing negative self-talk with positive self-talk.

Negative: *I'm not smart enough. I don't know what I'm doing.*

Positive: *I am enough. I can learn new things. My gifts will make room for me.*

Negative: *I'm too scared.*

Positive: *My doubts don't negate my talent. I grow more confident each day.*

Negative: *What if I fail?*

Positive: *It takes courage just to try. And what if I'm a smashing success? I am destined for greatness.*

Negative: *People like me don't belong here.*

Positive: *I belong here. I have the right to take up space. It's okay if I'm the first–I am a trailblazer!*

CHARACTER CONNECTION

Considering what we like about a fictional character can give us clues to positive traits we'd like to celebrate and cultivate in ourselves.

Think of a character you like from television, movies, or books, then answer the following questions:

Character: _____

What traits do you admire most about this character?

_____

_____

Why?

_____

_____

What positive traits do you have in common?

_____

_____

How can you use these strengths in a situation you're currently facing?

_____

_____

_____

_____

_____

_____

_____

_____

_____

_____

_____

_____

WEEK 22

Go on, brag a little! What makes you unique? What do you like most about yourself? What would other people be surprised to learn about you?

_____

_____

_____

_____

_____

What parts of yourself did you have trouble appreciating when you were younger, but you've now come to appreciate? What are you learning to like about yourself now?

_____

_____

_____

_____

_____

_____

SMELLY BUSINESS

Aromatherapy can support your journey to self-love.

Just prior to your meditation, or anytime you need a boost, add a few drops of a pure essential oil to a diffuser and let the scent fill the room, or inhale it from a cotton ball with a few drops on it.

Some scents can evoke different feelings, for example:

- Rose: self-love, compassion, soothing anxiousness

- Bergamot: joy, confidence, self-esteem

- Geranium: trust, healing from a broken heart

- Patchouli: grounding, balancing emotions, relaxation

BE YOUR OWN BEST FRIEND

The qualities you value in a close friend are just as valuable to give to yourself. Use this worksheet to reveal ways you can provide these qualities to yourself.

Consider the most important qualities you look for in a close friend—trust, honesty, kindness, fun, dependability, love, etc.—then choose your top three to complete the worksheet.

Quality	Why This Matters to Me	Ways I Can Offer This to Myself
Example: **Honesty**	**I want to trust that I have a friend who will tell me the truth, even if it's something I might not want to hear.**	**1. Be honest with myself and say no when I'm invited to an event I don't really want to go to. 2. Journal how I truly feel about my friendship with Keisha.**
1.		
2.		
3.		

WEEK 23

I have unlimited potential. I can be,
do, or have anything I want.

Think about the times you feel most confident. What are you most proud of yourself for? What would you like to feel more confident about?

_____

_____

_____

_____

_____

Reflect on the times you feel most doubtful. What thoughts or beliefs stand in the way of you feeling more confident? What would it take to truly believe in yourself?

_____

_____

_____

_____

_____

_____

CONFIDENT POSTURE

Posture isn't just noticed by others; it can also affect how you think about yourself. According to research, people who sit up straight feel more confident than those who tend to slump.

Be mindful of your posture when sitting, especially when looking down at your phone or laptop. If you notice you are slumping, adjust yourself by straightening your back, pulling both shoulders back, and distributing your body weight evenly on both hips.

LIKING HOW YOU LOOK

What do you like best about your appearance? Is it your smile? Your sense of style? Maybe you like your hair, your toes, or the curve of your eyebrows.

Complete the list below. If you get stuck, think of things a good friend would say they like about how you look.
Three things I like about how I look are:

1. _____

2. _____

3. _____

WEEK 24

I am open to new adventures, and I'm
willing to experience the world with
childlike wonder and curiosity.

Remember the adventures you dreamed of as a child. Does any
part of those dreams still resonate with you today? What's the
most adventurous thing you've done in your life so far?

_____

_____

_____

_____

_____

Think about the parts of your life that feel boring or uninspired.
What are three things you'd do if you weren't afraid? What are you
afraid will happen if you do them?

_____

_____

_____

_____

_____

SWITCH IT UP

Are you stuck on autopilot? Switching up your morning routine can help you get out of a rut and feel happier and more curious, even inspiring fresh solutions to old problems.

This week, switch up your routine in any way you can think of. Some ideas:

- If you typically shower before brushing your teeth, brush first.

- Take a different route to work or school.

- Style your hair differently or remix your outfits by pairing clothes with shoes or accessories you don't normally wear them with.

- Try a different flavor of coffee or jazz up your breakfast with a new recipe.

MAKE A BUCKET LIST

Creating a "bucket list" of things you want to experience is a great way to get clear about what you really want and stretch yourself beyond your comfort zone toward achieving your goals.

Complete these sentences:

1. A place I've always wanted to visit is _____

2. One activity I'd love to try is _____

3. As a child, I used to dream about doing _____

4. A food I've always wanted to try is _____

5. This might sound crazy, but what I really want to do one day is

_____

WEEK 25

Striving to grow or improve can be healthy; striving for perfection is not. In what ways might you demand perfectionism of yourself? Are those standards or expectations realistic? Why or why not?

_____

_____

_____

_____

_____

As a child, what happened if you made a mistake or didn't meet someone's expectations? How does that influence your choices today? If you were "perfect," what would you gain? What would you get to avoid?

_____

_____

_____

_____

_____

ACCEPT YOURSELF

1. Take three deep cleansing breaths.

2. Place your hand over your heart and repeat these words:

I don't need to be perfect to be loved and accepted. I am worthy of love just as I am. I am human, and I am allowed to make mistakes. I now commit to loving myself through my faults and mistakes. I am learning and growing. As I know better, I do better. I love me. I love and accept myself, now, today, without conditions.

INSPIRING STICKIES

Recall sayings you've heard that are "self-love affirmations" or "encouraging quotes." Search online if you need help. Write down any that resonate with you here:

1. _____

2. _____

3. _____

4. _____

5. _____

Choose a few of your favorites, write each one on a sticky note, and post them around your home or office to encourage and inspire you—don't forget to post one on your mirror! Say them out loud.

WEEK 26

Each day I find new reasons and ways
to love myself. I see my worth.

Kudos! You're halfway through your year of self-love! What have you learned about yourself and self-love so far? What has shifted for you? What would you like to celebrate?

_____

_____

_____

_____

_____

What parts of self-love feel challenging for you? Did you skip or avoid any uncomfortable topics in this journal? If so, which ones? If a loved one was halfway to accomplishing an important personal goal, what words of encouragement would you offer them?

_____

_____

_____

_____

_____

HONOR YOUR PROGRESS

It's an important self-love practice not only to celebrate completion of a goal, but also to celebrate your progress along the way. You deserve it! What would you like to do to honor your efforts and progress? Use this practice to figure it out.

1. Take a few deep, slow breaths.

2. Next, check in with your heart. Place both hands over your heart and ask: *Heart, how would you like to honor us and our progress?*

3. Pause and wait for the answer. Don't edit or second-guess it.

4. Then, do it!

HALFTIME CHECK-IN

Check in with yourself, and explore some things you've learned during this process so far. Complete the statements below:

1. An *a-ha* moment I've had when journaling is

   _____

2. I will seek help or support with

   _____

3. A practice or exercise I really enjoyed was

   _____

4. An area of myself I'd like to work on is

   _____

5. I'm seeing growth in the area of

_____

Reflections about my progress so far:

_____

_____

_____

_____

_____

_____

_____

_____

_____

WEEK 27

Our wants naturally evolve as we evolve. We aren't the same person we were ten or even two years ago. What previous goals or aspirations no longer fit who you are today? What is more important now?

_____

_____

_____

_____

_____

What thoughts or beliefs cause you to hesitate about changing your mind? Who could you be and what could you do if those thoughts and beliefs weren't true?

_____

_____

_____

_____

_____

ALIGN YOUR SPACE WITH YOUR DESIRES

Your surroundings can help or hinder the changes you want to make.

At home, notice any photos, artwork, or mementos that represent what you used to want and who you used to be. How do you feel when you encounter them? Consider replacing those with inspiring items that represent who you're becoming.

WHAT I REALLY WANT

Imagine being free of any guilt, other people's expectations, and concerns about time and money—past, present, or future. Write down what you really want in each area of your life:

Family: _____

Friendships: _____

Career: _____

Hobbies/Interests: _____

Home: _____

Health: _____

Relationship/Marriage: _____

Aspirations/Dreams: _____

Other: _____

WEEK 28

Peace is more than a moment or mood; it's a way of life. When and where do you feel most at peace? What does peace look and feel like for you?

_____

_____

_____

_____

_____

Think about the people and situations that add peace to your life, and those that disrupt your peace. How might you set boundaries with the latter?

_____

_____

_____

_____

_____

_____

FIVE SENSES MINDFULNESS

Focusing on your five senses shifts your attention away from stressors to peace.

1. Take a few deep, cleansing breaths. Be present in your surroundings.

2. Notice:
   5 things you see, such as a poster on your wall.
   4 things you hear—for example, the hum of a fan.
   3 things you feel, like a breeze or your feet touching the floor.
   2 things you smell, such as the lingering scent of soap on your hands.
   1 thing you taste—perhaps the coffee you just drank.

PRIORITIZING PEACE

On a scale of 1 to 5, indicate how peaceful you felt each day. Describe any instances when you intentionally chose peace.

	Very Peaceful	Neutral	Very Stressed	I chose peace by ...
Sun	1 2	3	4 5	
Mon	1 2	3	4 5	

Tues	1	2	3	4	5	
Wed	1	2	3	4	5	
Thurs	1	2	3	4	5	
Fri	1	2	3	4	5	
Sat	1	2	3	4	5	

Reflections about my peace of mind this week: _____

_____

_____

_____

_____

_____

WEEK 29

I am strong and capable. I can keep
trying even when things are hard.

Sometimes the only way out of difficult situations is to go *through*
them, and even the most successful people have felt defeated or
discouraged at times. What's going on in your life that's causing
frustration or sadness?

_____

_____

_____

_____

_____

What coping strategies have helped you get through difficult
times in the past? What are some things you can look forward to
when this situation is finally over (even if you don't know when or
how it will end)?

_____

_____

_____

_____

_____

COLLECT YOUR KUDOS

Create a paper or electronic collection of feel-good reminders of what you've accomplished and how you've impacted others. When you face a setback or feel discouraged, pull out your kudos and remind yourself how awesome you are!

In a box or in a computer file, collect things that make you feel good. Here are some types of things that might go in your kudos collection:

- A praise email from your boss
- Love letters
- A photo or screenshot of a work project you're proud of
- Compliments
- Greeting cards with meaningful notes inside
- Customer testimonials
- A photo of you receiving an award
- Thank-you notes

Reflect on others you could add.

WHAT'S GOING RIGHT

When we're facing a difficult time, it's easy to focus on what's going wrong. To keep things in perspective, brainstorm a list of anything that's going *right* in your life. These can be big things or small things—everything counts!

List things that are going well for you:

1. _____

2. _____

Continued→

3. _____

4. _____

5. _____

6. _____

7. _____

8. _____

9. _____

10. _____

11. _____

12. _____

WEEK 30

I am doing the best that I can. I can give myself care
and compassion even when I feel overwhelmed.

What are you juggling right now? Write everything down here. What
thoughts come up when you read through the list? What does it
feel like to have this much on your plate?

_____

_____

_____

_____

_____

Although we tend to want to do more when we feel overwhelmed,
doing less is sometimes the most loving choice for us. Does
the thought of doing less make you feel more anxious, or
relieved? Why?

_____

_____

_____

_____

_____

CONNECT WITH NATURE

One of the quickest ways to interrupt stressful thoughts is to connect with nature.

This week, get outside. The fresh air and some greenery will do you good. Go for a walk in the park or on a trail. Eat a picnic lunch. Hug a tree. Fish in a local pond. If you aren't able to get outside at all, simply gazing at a photo or screensaver of trees can help you feel calmer.

GET CLEAR ABOUT PRIORITIES

This exercise is inspired by an illustration by Liz Fosslein and will help you set clear priorities.

1. Write down everything on your to-do list in the column on the left.

2. Review the list and place each item from there onto a new list in the column on the right.

To Do List
_____
_____

Things I Have to Do
_____
_____

Things I Want to Do

Things Other People Want Me to Do

_____
_____

_____
_____

3. Eliminate or ignore nearly all the Things Other People Want Me to Do, and focus on one item at a time from the Things I Have to Do and Things I Want to Do lists.

WEEK 31

The more gratitude we feel, the more we receive to be grateful for. What do you appreciate most about your life? Whom or what do you sometimes take for granted?

_____

_____

_____

_____

_____

_____

What talents or personality traits are you most grateful for? What about yourself have you grown to appreciate over time?

_____

_____

_____

_____

_____

_____

GRATITUDE BREATH

1. Sit or lie in a comfortable position and focus on your breathing.

2. Reflect on something you are truly grateful for. If nothing specific comes to mind, reflect on being grateful for life itself.

3. As you breathe deeply and slowly, allow the feeling of gratitude to slowly spread from your heart throughout your body.

4. With each inhale, say in your mind, *I breathe in love.*

5. With every exhale, say in your mind, *I breathe out gratitude.*

FIVE-MINUTE GRATITUDE BLAST

Gratitude is one of the highest-vibration energies there is. Even just five minutes of feeling appreciation can have lasting effects.

Set a timer for five minutes, then brainstorm a list of everything you can think of that you're grateful for below.

_____

_____

_____

_____

_____

_____

As you move through this week, look for new opportunities to practice gratitude.

WEEK 32

What makes you feel loved? Describe specific actions and words that make you feel loved. How can you use these actions and words with yourself?

_____

_____

_____

_____

_____

Recall the most romantic experience you've ever had, in as much detail as you can remember. What made it so special? How would you characterize the current state of your love life?

_____

_____

_____

_____

_____

_____

WRITE YOURSELF A LOVE LETTER

1. Find a quiet space and write a handwritten love letter or love note to yourself.

2. Tell yourself how wonderful you are, including at least two specific things you love about yourself. Perhaps recall a favorite memory.

3. For an extra touch, before you begin writing, set the mood with a scented candle or some sweet-smelling incense.

4. Tuck the letter under your pillow and read it out loud before you go to bed.

ROMANCE YOURSELF BINGO

No matter your relationship status, the relationship with yourself is the foundation for your relationship with others. Your love life starts with you!

Mark each box on the next page to indicate it is a way you've romanced yourself. If you get five in a row, BINGO!

Take yourself out on a date	Write or recite a love poem	Buy yourself flowers or candy	Make yourself a playlist of love songs	Flirt with yourself in the mirror
Clean up your space for company (you!)	Whisper sweet affirmations to yourself	Go see a romantic movie	Wear something sexy just for yourself	Use the good sheets on your bed
Treat yourself to a massage or pampering session	Get a fresh hair style or cut	FREE SPACE	Buy yourself a special gift	Write yourself a love letter
Slow dance with yourself	Engage in self-pleasure	Celebrate the anniversary of a date you did something great	Tell a friend how excited you are about yourself	Cook a romantic meal
Admire a photo of yourself	Wear perfume or cologne	Take a romantic bath by candlelight	Give yourself a cute nickname	Go on a romantic getaway for a day or a weekend

WEEK 33

I am entitled to have a happy life. Limitless
bliss and joy are my birthrights.

What are some little things that make you happy? What made you
smile today? What or who is a regular source of joy in your life?

_____

_____

_____

_____

_____

When was the last time you were so engaged with what you were
doing that you lost track of time? Describe the experience. How
can you bring more of that activity or energy into your life on a
regular basis?

_____

_____

_____

_____

_____

_____

SELF-LOVE JAR

1. Fill sheets of paper with your favorite affirmations and short self-love quotes, leaving a bit of space around each one.

2. Cut the affirmations and quotes into individual strips or squares, and fold each one.

3. Place them in a jar with a lid.

4. Each day, pull an affirmation from the jar and read it out loud.

COLOR ME RELAXED

Coloring isn't just for children! It has many benefits for adults, too, including reducing stress and improving focus.

Color the design below. Feel free to color outside the lines or embellish it with added decorations if you like!

WEEK 34

I am my ancestors' wildest dream! I draw upon the
wisdom and strength of those who came before me.

Does your family, faith, or culture have any traditions that honor
loved ones who have passed on? What are they? Do you feel connected to your ancestors or these practices? Why or why not?

_____

_____

_____

_____

_____

Knowing yourself as you do, what do you think your ancestors
were like? What do you picture being their strengths? Weak-
nesses? How do these traits impact your personality and values?

_____

_____

_____

_____

_____

_____

REMEMBER YOUR ANCESTORS

A simple act of remembrance can create a powerful connection between you and family members who came before you, even if you've never met.

Reflect on how you'd like to honor your ancestors. If your culture or faith has specific traditions, you could draw from those. Other ideas include:

- Light a candle dedicated to your ancestors.

- Hang a photo of a deceased loved one.

- Cook a meal using recipes passed down in your family. If you like, you could also invite family elders to join you at a family gathering.

- Ask family elders about their earliest family memories, family values, or traditions. You can listen, write their responses, or even videotape the conversation if they're okay with it.

MY ANCESTORS AND ME

Have you ever wondered about your ancestors' lives, and what it might be like to get to know each other? Complete the following statements below:

If I could, I would ask my ancestors _____

_____

_____

_____

I wonder what my ancestors would think about _____

_____

_____

If I could, I would thank my ancestors for _____

_____

_____

_____

_____

I wish my ancestors knew that I _____

_____

_____

_____

_____

The ancestor I'd most like to meet is _____

because _____

_____

_____

_____

If I knew my ancestors could help me, I'd ask them for help with:

_____

_____

_____

_____

WEEK 35

The way we feel about ourselves often starts with how our family viewed us. How would the family you grew up in describe you? Was this narrative ever true for you? Why or why not? If yes, is it still true now?

_____

_____

_____

_____

_____

What physical characteristics, personality traits, talents, or habits that run in your family are you proud of? Are there any multi-generational patterns of dysfunction you are determined not to repeat? What will you choose to do differently?

_____

_____

_____

_____

_____

SHAKE IT OFF

It's important to move tension, fear, and stuck energy out of your body. One way to do this is to shake things up!

While standing, hold your arms out at your sides with your hands hanging loosely at your wrists. Begin shaking both hands vigorously, as if you were shaking water off them. After ten seconds, gradually expand the shaking to include your arms, then shoulders, then head, torso, and legs, until you're shaking your entire body. Shake your whole body for a count of ten, then be still. Take three deep, cleansing breaths, focusing on exhaling any remaining tension in your body.

DESCRIBE YOUR FAMILY

Being aware of what you've experienced in life can help you get clear about what you want to create going forward.

1. With a pen or pencil, circle the five words that best describe the emotional environment within your immediate family while growing up:

abusive	fun	needy	stable
absent	ideal	nonexistent	strained
authoritarian	kind	nurturing	strict
celebratory	judgmental	progressive	supportive
chaotic	lenient	reserved	tolerant
close-knit	loving	resilient	traditional
competitive	mutually-	responsible	unstable
detached	respectful	restrictive	welcoming
distant	open	rigid	
encouraging	ostracizing	sappy	
favoritism-prone	overbearing	secretive	
	protective	sentimental	

Or, add your own words here:

_____

_____

_____

_____

2. With a highlighter or brightly colored pen, mark the five words that describe the emotional environment you'd like to cultivate within your biological or chosen family.

WEEK 36

I enjoy my body, and I am entitled to
discover all the pleasure it holds.

What were the attitudes about sexual pleasure in your family
growing up? What, if anything, were you taught about your
body and about self-pleasure? By whom? What do you wish you
were taught?

_____

_____

_____

_____

_____

How would you describe your current relationship with your body?
How can you be a better lover to yourself? What do you need to
feel sexy, safe, and comfortable?

_____

_____

_____

_____

_____

EXPLORING SOLO PLEASURE

Learning how to please yourself without guilt or shame is import-ant, regardless of whether you engage in partnered sex. Make a pleasure date with yourself!

1. Set a sexy mood with lighting, candles, and music.

2. Whether you're new to it or well-practiced, touch your body without attachment to any particular outcome.

3. Be guided simply by what feels good to you and notice the different sensations that different kinds of touches create.

WHAT TURNS YOU ON?

Explore what you find sexy about yourself by filling in the blanks below:

1. The sexiest thing about me is _____

   _____

2. I really turned myself on when _____

3. The most sensitive part of my body is _____

4. One thing I'd like to try is _____

   _____

WEEK 37

I am worthy of my own love. I make
the time to love myself well.

What does unconditional self-love look like to you? How often do
you engage in activities that are designed simply to respond to
your needs? If not daily, what do you think stands in your way?

_____

_____

_____

_____

_____

Do you ever feel guilty for treating yourself well? If so, what
thoughts and beliefs come up? What language could you use with
yourself instead?

_____

_____

_____

_____

_____

_____

WHAT'S MY SELF-LOVE LANGUAGE?

The intention of Gary Chapman's popular book *The 5 Love Languages* was to help people improve their relationships by learning their mate's "love language"–the most meaningful ways they recognize and receive love. However, the same language you use to give love to and receive love from others can be used to love *yourself*!

What's your default love language? Words of affirmation, acts of service, receiving gifts, physical touch, or quality time? Take the 5 Love Languages Quiz online at 5LoveLanguages.com/quizzes /love-language.

SELF-LOVE TO-DO LIST

Using your love language is a great way to love yourself!

From the list below, check off the ones that resonate with you. Choose three items from the list that you'll do this week, or make up your own.

Acts of Self-Service: Making your life easier

_____ Ask for help   _____ Order dinner delivery

_____ Declutter a junk drawer   _____ Organize photos

_____ Get a babysitter   _____ Get therapy

_____ Hire a housekeeper

Quality Time: Spending time with yourself alone, doing things you love

_____ Engage in hobbies   _____ Meditate

_____ Make art   _____ Read or listen to a book

_____ Sleep in

_____ Take a long walk

_____ Sit in nature

_____ Take yourself on a date

_____ Spend a solo night
in a hotel

Physical Touch: Making your body feel good; pursuing physical well-being

_____ Bathe/soak

_____ Get or give yourself a
manicure/pedicure

_____ Wear cozy, soft clothes

_____ Get a massage

_____ Cuddle with a pet

_____ Engage in Reiki healing

_____ Exercise

_____ Cuddle under a
weighted blanket

_____ Enjoy a facial

_____ Play with a fidget spinner

_____ Do yoga or stretch

Receiving Gifts: Buying or making yourself gifts

_____ Paint rocks with inspiring
messages

_____ Order a monthly
subscription box

_____ Buy some craft supplies

_____ Paint a canvas in colors
that please you

_____ Plant or give your-
self flowers

_____ Shop for a new outfit or
accessory

_____ Invest in your dream

_____ Book a trip (or plan one
for the future!)

_____ Treat yourself to your
favorite meal

_____ Make yourself
some jewelry

Words of Affirmation: Speaking positive and encouraging words to yourself

_____ Say affirmations out loud

_____ Journal

_____ Play uplifting music (page 62)

_____ Engage in positive self-talk

_____ Post positive quotes on your mirror

_____ Watch an inspiring sermon or talk

_____ Read your kudos collection (page 85)

_____ Write yourself a love letter

The three I will use to love myself this week are:

1. _____

2. _____

3. _____

WEEK 38

I listen to my heart and trust it to lead the way.

How comfortable do you feel allowing your heart to guide you? Have you ever felt that your own heart betrayed you? If so, how?

_____

_____

_____

_____

_____

_____

Describe a time when you trusted your heart and things worked out for the better. What might change for you if you trusted yourself completely all the time?

_____

_____

_____

_____

_____

_____

AUDIO MEDITATION

Your ears could be the key to a more peaceful, more open heart. This week, try tuning into some self-loving meditations.

Find a quiet space, sit or lie comfortably, and listen to an audio meditation for healing or opening the heart chakra. Chakras are energy centers in the body. Listen with headphones if you need to minimize outside noise or distractions. (You can find many free mediations of various lengths on YouTube or meditation apps like Insight Timer or Headspace.)

A HEARTFELT YES

Get into the habit of checking in with your heart. Try to do this exercise earlier in your day.

What are seven things your heart wants to say YES to today? Don't overthink or edit. Write them here:

1. _____

2. _____

3. _____

4. _____

5. _____

6. _____

7. _____

WEEK 39

Are you growing more confident in some areas since you began using this journal? If so, what are they, and what has changed? When or how did you notice the shift?

_____

_____

_____

_____

_____

In what ways do you doubt yourself? What area do you want to feel more sure about? What words could you use to encourage yourself while moving through these doubts?

_____

_____

_____

_____

_____

_____

STRONG LIKE A TREE

When you aren't feeling confident or strong, you can borrow strength from nature.

1. Outside, find a tree with the largest, sturdiest trunk.

2. With your back to the tree, stand as close to it as you can.

3. Lean back against the tree, with as much as your torso and bottom touching it as possible, allowing the tree to support your body weight.

4. Take five deep, slow breaths.

5. As you breathe in, draw strength from the tree, feel how the tree supports you and has your back. As you breathe out, offer appreciation to the tree.

6. Continue until you feel calmer and more grounded.

THIRD-QUARTER CHECK-IN

Check in with yourself and your journey since you began using this journal. Complete the statements below:

1. Some progress that I can celebrate is _____

_____

2. An eye-opening journaling exercise was _____

_____

3. Something I'm really curious about right now is _____

_____

4. I can be more patient with myself with _____

_____

WEEK 40

I release the need to control outcomes. I trust
that everything is working out for me.

What do you feel anxious about today? What would your day be
like if you didn't have any of these feelings? What are some things
you can do to take charge of how you feel?

_____

_____

_____

_____

_____

Describe a time you were successful in spite of feeling anxious.
What did you tell yourself in order to move forward? What factors
led to your success?

_____

_____

_____

_____

_____

_____

BUTTERFLY HUG

When feeling anxious or overwhelmed, you can activate energy points on your body to feel more calm.

1. Take a few deep, slow cleansing breaths.

2. Cross your arms across your chest, resting your hands on your shoulders or upper arms.

3. Gently tap your hands, alternating left and right and tapping ten times each.

4. Repeat for sixty seconds or until you feel more grounded and calm. As you do, continue to breathe deeply and slowly.

ILLUSTRATE THE FEELING

Draw, paint, color, or paste an image of what anxiety feels like, and what calm feels like, in the areas below.

Anxiety:

Calm:

WEEK 41

Write about a mistake you made recently. What happened? What thoughts came up, and how did you treat yourself when you realized the mistake? Did your response feel more like punishment or encouragement? Why?

_____

_____

_____

_____

_____

Describe something valuable you learned from a past mistake. Knowing that mistakes are learning opportunities, what are some specific ways you can offer yourself more compassion the next time you make one?

_____

_____

_____

_____

_____

POSITIVE REPLAY

The words you think and speak to yourself are powerful.

Choose any three positive affirmations that resonate with you and write them down. Make an audio recording of yourself reading the affirmations out loud. Try using the voice memo function on your phone, or call your own voicemail and leave a voice message for yourself. Listen to the recording each day this week and save it to replay whenever you're having a tough day.

USE YOUR STRENGTHS

Focusing on your strengths helps build self-esteem, and creating a plan to use them can help you increase your success and confidence.

Write three of your strengths. (Examples: creativity, honesty, resourcefulness)

1. _____

2. _____

3. _____

Map out a plan for how you will use your strengths this week. Put a star next to each action item after you complete it.

	Strength	Action Plan	★
Ex: **Sun**	Creativity	**After brunch, I will start working on Li's costume for the recital.**	★
Sun			
Mon			
Tues			
Wed			
Thurs			
Fri			
Sat			

WEEK 42

I am worthy right now. I don't have to wait
until I achieve certain accomplishments
to love myself and enjoy my life.

Have you ever delayed something you would enjoy, or completely
turned down an opportunity, because you felt undeserving? If so,
describe it.

_____

_____

_____

_____

_____

What would you start doing today if you felt worthy of it? What
beliefs are holding you back? What would you need to believe is
true in order to start feeling worthy?

_____

_____

_____

_____

_____

_____

PIN A REMINDER

Create an affirmation that's meaningful to you, such as:

- It's safe to try something new.

- I deserve to have a good life.

- It's getting easier and easier to love myself.

Pin a safety pin on your clothes in a place where you can see it periodically, but that isn't very visible to others, such as the cuff of your shirtsleeve. Every time you see the pin, pause and repeat your affirmation three times.

IN MY LIFETIME . . .

Having a meaningful goal or aspiration can help connect you to your purpose and build your confidence as you get closer to achieving it.

Complete the worksheet below.

At the end of a long and healthy life . . .

. . . I would feel proud knowing that I had _____

_____.

. . . I would like to have made peace with_____

_____.

. . . I would feel content knowing that I had_____

_____

. . . I would most like to be remembered for_____

_____

WEEK 43

Abundance is my birthright!

What's your relationship like with money? When you experience financial stress, how do you handle it? When you have money, do you trust your ability to manage (or learn how to manage) it well?

_____

_____

_____

_____

_____

_____

What's one financial decision or situation that you're proud of? What would having more money represent to you (security, freedom, power, etc.)? What would it change for you?

_____

_____

_____

_____

_____

_____

RICH MONEY

Buy or create "rich money"–that is, paper currency in a high denomination, such as a million-dollar bill, or a metallic gold hundred-dollar bill. You can buy novelty money online or at a party supply store, or make your own. Keep it in your wallet, and every time you open it, look at your rich money and say, "Abundance is my birthright!"

LIMITING BELIEFS ABOUT MONEY

Growing your awareness of limiting beliefs about money can help you overcome them.

Place a check mark next to the statements below that you relate to:

___ Money doesn't grow on trees.

___ You have to work really hard to have a lot of money.

___ Wanting more money is greedy.

___ Money is the root of all evil.

___ I'll lose friends or loved ones if I make a lot of money (or if I don't have money).

___ Rich people are greedy or corrupt.

___ More money; more problems.

___ Wanting more money makes me less spiritual.

___ People like me can't make a lot of money.

How might the statements you checked affect your current relationship with money? _____

_____

_____

_____

_____.

The good news is you have the power to change your beliefs. Repeat "Abundance is my birthright!" every morning this week.

WEEK 44

Frequently comparing yourself to others can keep you from feeling worthy. If you tend to do this, when and where are you most likely to make such comparisons, and in what areas?

_____

_____

_____

_____

_____

What's the difference between envy and inspiration? Who do you admire, and why? What might you learn from them that you can use to inspire yourself as you pursue your own goals and dreams?

_____

_____

_____

_____

_____

SOCIAL MEDIA FAST

Social media is a leading culprit of self-comparison. Going on a social media fast—taking a break from all social media for a period of time—is a self-loving practice that can increase positivity, decrease anxiety, and relieve feelings of depression.

1. Set an intention for your fast. What are you hoping to accomplish? How long will you fast? A week? Longer?

2. Give your friends a heads-up that they won't be able to reach you that way, and let select people know how they can connect with you offline.

3. Turn off all push notifications for your social media accounts. Consider removing those apps from your phone so you aren't tempted to open them during your fast. (Don't worry, you can reinstall them later.)

4. When you feel the urge to use social media, check in with yourself by asking: *Why do I want to open it? Out of boredom? To engage? To ease the feeling that I'm missing out on something? To get approval or attention?* Journal about your feelings. What action can you take instead of logging on?

When you're ready to return, be mindful of how you consume this media. Unfollow any social media accounts that make you feel bad about yourself. Choose to follow accounts that inspire and uplift you.

OWN YOUR AWESOME

Staying focused on your own goals and progress is key to staying out of the self-comparison trap.

Complete the sentences below to remind yourself how awesome you are!

Something I do really well is _____

_____.

Three things I'm grateful for are: _____

_____.

I'm proud of myself for _____

_____.

My secret talent is _____

_____.

My favorite positive word or phrase to describe myself is _____

_____.

WEEK 45

I forgive myself for any hurt I've caused myself
and others. In doing so, I free myself from the
burden of guilt and shame. I love all parts of me.

What do you blame yourself for? Write it all down, without over-thinking or editing. How does carrying the burden of blame, guilt, or shame affect you?

_____

_____

_____

_____

_____

If you forgave yourself completely and released the past, where would you be in one year? If you held on to the guilt and the shame, where would you be a year from now? How can you offer yourself more compassion about it today?

_____

_____

_____

_____

_____

A GOOD CRY

Sometimes we just need a good cry. Tears are hurt on the inside coming out to be healed and released. Crying is not weakness; your tears are cleansing.

1. Choose a private space at home, out in nature, or anywhere else you feel safe and comfortable.

2. Take several deep breaths and allow yourself to feel whatever emotions come up: sadness, frustration, grief, shame, disappointment, fear, heartbreak, etc.

3. Be fully present to the feelings you're releasing as you weep, sob, or wail.

4. Journal about it.

   Afterward, consider a gentle, comforting activity, such as a warm bath, a nap, or some stretching. Be gentle with yourself today.

FREEDOM THROUGH FORGIVENESS

When we forgive, we liberate ourselves from the weight of the past. Forgiveness doesn't mean you condone what happened. Forgiveness says, "I'm ready to surrender the burden of this."

Complete these sentences:

I forgive myself for _____

_____.

I forgive myself for _____

_____.

I forgive myself for _____

_____.

I am not quite ready to forgive myself for _____

_____.

I am not quite ready to forgive myself for _____

_____.

I am not quite ready to forgive myself for _____

_____.

I forgive _____ for _____

_____.

I forgive _____ for _____

_____.

I forgive _____ for _____

_____.

One day I'll be ready to forgive _____ for _____

_____.

One day I'll be ready to forgive _____ for _____

_____.

One day I'll be ready to forgive _____ for _____

_____.

WEEK 46

Think about a time when you felt brave. What was the situation?
Describe how you summoned your courage or where it came from.
What did you learn from that experience?

_____

_____

_____

_____

_____

Courage is something we need to tackle the challenges in life. Is
there any issue, task, or person you're avoiding because you feel
intimidated or afraid? What encouragement can you give yourself
to face this challenge?

_____

_____

_____

_____

_____

BIGGER AND SMALLER

Sometimes fear can make a situation seem bigger than it is. Let's practice shrinking fear to a more realistic size.

1. In your mind, visualize a horse.

2. Imagine it growing until it is the size of a house.

3. Next, shrink the horse down to its original size, then smaller still, until it fits in the palm of your hand.

4. Say out loud: *I can use the power of my mind to keep any problem in its proper perspective.*

ME, SUPERHERO

If you could be your own superhero, what superpower or special ability would you have? What would you call yourself? _____

_____

How did you come to get these powers? _____

_____.

Is there anything special you need to do to activate your special powers? If so, what? _____

_____

_____.

What does your costume look like? Do you carry any special tools?

_____

_____

_____.

Draw your superhero costume and accessories here:

WEEK 47

I release the need to be liked by everyone. I
am enough, and I am pleasing to myself.

Are you doing anything you don't want to do because you are
afraid of displeasing someone? What is it? What emotions come
up when you think about doing this? What does it feel like in
your body?

_____

_____

_____

_____

_____

What's one thing you are afraid people will think about you? What
would change for you if you no longer cared what anybody else
thought? How would it feel?

_____

_____

_____

_____

_____

SET AN ENERGY INTENTION

1. Choose a word that describes the mood or energy you want to create for yourself this week–for example, joy, peace, confident, fun, connected, grounded, abundant, light, ease, calm, relaxed, curious, adventurous, winning, etc.

2. Each morning this week, connect with your intention to create this feeling in your life.

3. Throughout the day, observe when this energy shows up, and make a mental note or write it in your journal. When you need to make a decision, ask yourself what choice would this energy make? For instance, *What would adventure do in this situation?*

PEOPLE-PLEASING RED FLAGS

Circle True or False for each statement below:

1. I like to get a lot of opinions from other people before I make a decision. **True / False**

2. I allow someone to keep saying or doing things that hurt me because I don't want to lose them. **True / False**

3. I usually pretend I'm okay even when I'm not. **True / False**

4. Sometimes I change myself to fit in or meet someone else's expectations. **True / False**

5. I frequently allow someone else's opinions to become my opinions. **True / False**

6. It's common for me to agree with people because I want them to like me, even if I really disagree. **True / False**

7. I often say yes to someone, then end up resenting them later. **True / False**

8. I tend to stay quiet about what's bothering me because I don't want to rock the boat. **True / False**

9. I sometimes lend people money even when I can't pay all of my own bills. **True / False**

10. I usually feel responsible for keeping other people happy. **True / False**

# of True Statements: _____

If you answered True for:

2 or fewer: People-pleasing isn't a dominant issue for you, but it's helpful to check in with yourself about what's underneath any statement to which you answered True.

3 to 6: Your sense of self-worth is somewhat dependent on other people. Working with this journal can help you build confidence and discover ways to love yourself that don't have anything to do with others.

7 or more: You're likely at the beginning of your self-love journey, but you're in the right place. As you work through the reflective prompts and practices in this journal, consider enlisting the help of a therapist or other qualified counselor to support you along the way.

WEEK 48

Describe a difficult life event that ultimately had a positive impact on who you are today. How did you get through the roughest parts of it? Can those methods help you at this time?

_____

_____

_____

_____

_____

How can you show kindness to yourself while you're in a difficult time? If a loved one was feeling discouraged, in what specific ways would you offer support? Which way feels most soothing to you right now?

_____

_____

_____

_____

_____

HONOR YOUR FEELINGS

When you feel like you just can't get your act together, be gentle with yourself. Here are some self-loving messages to help you find a little peace amid the turmoil.

1. Take three deep, slow breaths. Place your hand over your heart and say this out loud:

   It is okay to feel afraid, exhausted, stressed, overwhelmed, broken, weak, uncertain, doubtful, not together, imperfect, too late, disconnected, stuck, not smart enough, empty, wrong, alone, not strong enough, like a fraud, messy, out of alignment, not pretty enough, depressed, and way behind.

   It is okay to feel terrified, busted, not chosen, not cut out for this, invisible, ill, misunderstood, falling apart, not trusting, not trustworthy, powerless, confused, not belonging, disappointed, lonely, uncomfortable, not healthy enough, broke, unworthy, and like I just can't get it right.

   It is okay to feel small, timid, unkempt, heartbroken, off balance, not good enough, exposed, unwanted, foolish, anxious, unlovable, unlucky, angry, regretful, inadequate, like a failure. It is okay to feel this way right now. My feelings are valid.

2. Now say:

   These are feelings. These are stories. These are things I feel, but they are not who I am. These are feelings, not truths, and this is not where my story ends! I love and accept myself through all of it.

CELEBRATE ALL THE WINS

Celebrating the good things happening in our lives can help us keep perspective when it feels like everything is going wrong.

Brainstorm below all the ways you could celebrate a victory or positive development, no matter how small.

Examples:
Meet up with a friend for a celebratory toast.
Place gold star stickers all over my mirror.

_____

_____

_____

_____

_____

_____

_____

_____

_____

_____

_____

_____

_____

_____

_____

_____

WEEK 49

Are you comfortable accepting compliments—able to receive one
and fully bask in it without immediately returning a compliment
right back to the person? Why or why not?

_____

_____

_____

_____

_____

What are the best three compliments you have ever received?
What words from others made you light up inside? What compliments would you give yourself?

_____

_____

_____

_____

_____

_____

QIGONG INNER SMILE MEDITATION

Qigong, pronounced "chee gung," is a Chinese wellness practice that combines breathwork, movement, and mindfulness. The Inner Smile meditation promotes relaxation, joy, and self-love.

1. Sit comfortably and close your eyes.

2. Slow your breathing, relaxing your body with each breath.

3. Visualize a peaceful, joyful image or memory, such as a child laughing or a beautiful flower. Allow that mental image to bring a smile to your lips.

4. Send the smile inward into your body, visualizing the smile moving through your body, growing bigger as it enters all of your organs, muscles, and bones.

5. Give thanks for and to your body. Give thanks for your heart.

6. Continue to sit and breathe, feeling your entire body smiling for several minutes.

HYPE INTRODUCTION

Write a "hype introduction" for yourself that includes a fun nickname and touts something you want to accomplish in the future. Dream big–the more outrageous, the better! Don't be afraid to brag or hype yourself up, and be sure to add your favorite exclamation or audience reaction at the end.

Fill in these blanks:

Your first name: _____

_____.

Something you want to own or do: _____

_____.

Your last name: _____

_____.

Something you really want to accomplish: _____

_____.

Something fun or silly you want to accomplish: _____

_____.

Something outrageous you want to accomplish: _____

_____.

Favorite exclamation or audience reaction: _____

_____.

Next, write your hype introduction:

Examples:

Introducing . . . Jamila "J-Billions" White, *New York Times* bestselling author and professional beach goddess! *cheers and applause*

Introducing . . . Osei "Slam Dunk" Titus, chess grand master, illustrator for Marvel's latest superhero saga, and discoverer of the cure for lactose intolerance! Booyah!

Your turn!

Introducing . . .

_____

_____

_____

_____

_____

_____

_____

_____

_____

_____

_____

_____

_____

_____

_____

_____

_____

_____

_____

_____

_____

Now, read it out loud in a big voice, with all the sound effects!

WEEK 50

Endless possibilities surround me. I am
inspired by all that life has to offer.

Hope and motivation are healthy indicators of self-esteem. Who
or what truly inspires you? What are you most looking forward to
right now?

_____

_____

_____

_____

_____

What energizes you? Write about a time you felt uninspired or
unmotivated. How did you get over the hump? How did you find
your motivation again?

_____

_____

_____

_____

_____

PEP TALK

Boost your confidence and motivation by giving yourself a pep talk. What words do you most need to hear to encourage and inspire yourself? Here's an example:

"(Your name), you got this! You can do anything you set your mind to. I know you can do it. I believe in you, (name)! This day was made for you. You are destined to succeed. Your victory is already determined. You have everything you need within you to make it. Let's get it!"

ARTIST DATE

In a strategy borrowed from Julia Cameron's book *The Artist's Way*, let's embark on an artist date—that is, a lighthearted solo "date" you take yourself on to explore something that interests or inspires you.

Brainstorm a list of future artist dates you'd like to take yourself on. When you feel stuck or unmotivated, pull out this list, pick one thing, and do it.

Three places I used to love to go as a child are:

1. _____

2. _____

3. _____

As a child, I enjoyed myself so much I'd lose track of time

when I _____

_____.

A game I really loved to play as a child is _____
_____.

My favorite childhood toy or collection was _____
_____.

If I had a whole weekend afternoon to myself, I would _____
_____.

A store I'd love to lose myself in is _____
_____.

A live event I always wanted to watch is _____
_____.

I always wanted to take a class or workshop to learn how to _____
_____.

If I had the time, I'd love to make or play around with _____
_____.

I always wanted to go on a tour of _____
_____.

In nature, I am most inspired by _____
_____.

I felt so energized that time I went to _____
_____.

An exhibit I always wanted to see is _____
_____.

Other ideas for artist dates:

_____

_____

_____

_____

_____

_____

_____

_____

_____

_____

_____

_____

_____

_____

_____

_____

_____

_____

_____

_____

_____

_____

WEEK 51

I am finding my voice. I can speak my truth, even
if my voice quivers and my knees shake.

Were you ever reprimanded or ridiculed for speaking up?
Does that experience still impact you today? If so, in what
specific ways?

_____

_____

_____

_____

_____

What is something you need to say to someone that you haven't
said? Where in your body do you hold those unspoken or stuck
words? What would it feel like to be free of this burden?

_____

_____

_____

_____

_____

_____

ACTIVATE YOUR THROAT CHAKRA

Chakras are energy centers in the body. A balanced throat chakra allows you to express yourself with authenticity, giving "voice" to your feelings, thoughts, and ideas, even if you express them non-vocally, such as through music, art, or writing.

One way to activate your throat chakra is to use your vocal cords. Set your intention to open your throat chakra and spend five minutes each day this week doing one of these activities:

- Sing an empowering song

- Pray out loud

- Hum

- Chant *ham* (pronounced "hahm")

- Repeat affirmations out loud

- Whistle

SPEAKING YOUR TRUTH

Effectively using the power of your voice starts with being truthful with yourself.

Complete the sentences below:

If I am completely honest with myself, what I really need to get off

my chest is _____

_____.

What I truly want to say to _____ is

_____.

I'm afraid to tell anyone that _____

_____ .

Three things I know to be true about myself are:

1. _____

2. _____

3. _____

WEEK 52

Congratulations! How does it feel to reach week 52? What did you learn about yourself through this year of journaling? What specific shifts or changes have you noticed?

_____

_____

_____

_____

_____

How will you celebrate this important accomplishment? What specific steps will you take to continue your progress with loving yourself more fully? How will you get back on track when you feel discouraged?

_____

_____

_____

_____

_____

REWARD YOURSELF!

Completing this journal is a huge deal. Honor your commitment and your success by giving yourself a tangible reward.

With art supplies or a computer, make your own "Certificate of Completion." Make it fun and colorful!

Now, celebrate yourself with a special treat. You could take yourself out, or perhaps even share this victory with loved ones. You deserve it!

FINAL SELF-LOVE CHECK-IN

Circle the number that describes how much you disagree (0) or agree (5) with each statement below:

I really love myself.

0   1   2   3   4   5

I have many positive qualities.

0   1   2   3   4   5

I practice self-care regularly.

0   1   2   3   4   5

I feel worthy of love.

0   1   2   3   4   5

I am a good person.

0   1   2   3   4   5

I have the power to create positive change in my life.

0   1   2   3   4   5

I make good decisions.

0   1   2   3   4   5

I like how I look.

| 0 | 1 | 2 | 3 | 4 | 5 |

I honor and maintain healthy boundaries.

| 0 | 1 | 2 | 3 | 4 | 5 |

I deserve a good life.

| 0 | 1 | 2 | 3 | 4 | 5 |

I have healthy relationships.

| 0 | 1 | 2 | 3 | 4 | 5 |

Add up the total for every number circled.

TOTAL SCORE: _____

If you scored:

0 to 11: You have a great opportunity to start loving yourself and building up your sense of self-worth. Continued work with this journal will help you do just that. Revisit any weeks that resonate with you.

12 to 22: You're opening to self-love. Continued work with the practices in this book will help you gain self-confidence and become more aware of how to be more loving with yourself.

23 to 33: You're growing into a healthy relationship with yourself. An intentional and consistent self-love and self-care practice will help you strengthen it further.

34 or more: You're well connected to your heart and are loving yourself well. Keep going!

Now, compare your results from week 1 from page 5:

Week 1 total: _____

Week 52 total: _____

Reflections about your year of self-love: _____

_____

_____

_____

_____

_____

_____

_____

_____

_____

_____

_____

_____

_____

_____

_____

_____

_____

_____

A FINAL NOTE

CONGRATULATIONS, YOU DID IT!

Your completion of this journal is the beginning of a lifelong positive, loving relationship with yourself. I hope you are proud of yourself because I am certainly proud of you!

The understanding and discipline that you've gained through this process are invaluable. Don't stop now! Continue your journaling practice. Whether you revisit the affirmations, prompts, and other practices in this journal to help you stay focused, or you experiment with less structured journaling techniques, keep going! Your love for and belief in yourself can only grow stronger.

Also, by now, you've gotten some great insights into what works best for you. You can spot the things that might throw you off track with your practice, and address them or call in additional support.

Keep going.

You can do this.

You've already done it.

You are so worthy, and so worth it.

I wish you every joy in the next season of your self-love journey.

I love you.

RESOURCES

◇◇◇

For additional self-love resources from Jamila, including the support community of other like-hearted souls who are working in their *A Year of Self-Love Journals*, visit ayearofselflove.com

BOOKS AND CARD DECKS

The Artist's Way: A Spiritual Path to Higher Creativity by Julia Cameron

Codependent No More: How to Stop Controlling Others and Start Caring for Yourself by Melody Beattie

The Four Agreements: A Practical Guide to Personal Freedom by Don Miguel Ruiz

"Power Thought Cards: A 64-Card Deck" by Louise Hay

Set Boundaries, Find Peace: A Guide to Reclaiming Yourself by Nedra Glover Tawwab

ONLINE

YouTube Channel: Toni Jones

Music videos like "Energy Budget" offer affirmations on boundaries and self-worth.

SelfLoveRainbow.com

Downloads and printables on self-love, self-care, and mental health

REFERENCES

Bunch, Erin. "I'm a Psychologist, and These Are the Benefits of Taking a Social Media Fast." *Well+Good*. April 19, 2021. wellandgood.com/social-media-fast-benefits.

Calderon, Dominee. "The Self-Love Rainbow." *SelfLoveRainbow .com* (blog). February 15, 2017. selfloverainbow.com/2017 /02/5-self-love-languages.html.

Cameron, Julia. *The Artist's Way: A Spiritual Path to Higher Creativity*. New York: J.P. Tarcher/Putnam, 2002.

Fosslein, Liz (@lizandmollie). "To Set Better Boundaries." Instagram photo. June 15, 2022. instagram.com/p /Ce1T61YrXWB.

5 Love Languages Quiz. Based on the book "The 5 Love Languages: The Secret to Love that Lasts" by Gary Chapman. 5lovelanguages.com/quizzes/love-language.

Gulbrandsen, Britney. "Showing Love for Yourself: How to Practice Self-Love." *ColorMyHappy.com* (blog). February 10, 2018. colormyhappy.com/discovering-how-to-show-yourself-love.

Ohio State University. "Body Posture Affects Confidence in Your Own Thoughts, Study Finds." *ScienceDaily*. October 5, 2009. sciencedaily.com/releases/2009/10/091005111627.htm.

Therapist Aid (blog). "Strengths Use Plan." therapistaid.com/ therapy-worksheet/strengths-use-plan.

ACKNOWLEDGMENTS

The writing of this book took a little while, but the years of living guided what I wrote. My heart is so full of appreciation:

For Spirit: for my ancestors, angels, and guides, for whispering into my heart.

For my family: Mom, Dad, Lorraine, Sydnye, Whitney, Khari, Kach, Sanj, and Keeks.

For my clients and students, who turned out to be my teachers, leading me on a deeper journey into my own self-love. For A.D., who asked me the question that started it all. For the therapists, teachers, and coaches who have created safe spaces for me to work through the tricky bits over the years.

For my friends who listened, who believed. For my Sorors of Delta Sigma Theta and especially the ladies of Assiduous 40, spring '94, Alpha Chapter—my forever cheerleaders who have my back on every business, every crazy idea, and now every book.

For the team at Rockridge Press for putting amazing books out into the world, and for trusting me with this one. And especially to my editor Laura Cerrone for your encouragement and gentle questions.

And finally, for the island of Barbados and its people, for showing me new ways to love myself, and for being the beautiful container for my life and for the writing of this book.

I am so very grateful. For all of you. For all of it.

ABOUT THE AUTHOR

JAMILA I. WHITE is an internationally acclaimed psychic medium, life coach, and certified Reiki Master Teacher who empowers clients all over the world to love and trust themselves via private consultations, classes and group coaching, and transformational retreats.

A summa cum laude graduate of Howard University and member of Delta Sigma Theta Sorority, Inc., Jamila's home is by the sea in Barbados, where she is living her best life. Reach her on her website, www.jamilawhite.com, and on social media at @InspiredJamila (Facebook) and @Inspired.Jamila (Instagram).

CPSIA information can be obtained
at www.ICGtesting.com
Printed in the USA
JSHW071930120123
36199JS00004B/4